Holly,
Reindeer,
and Colored Lights

Other Clarion Books by Edna Barth

Jack-O'-Lantern

Hearts, Cupids, and Red Roses
The Story of the Valentine Symbols

Witches, Pumpkins, and Grinning Ghosts
The Story of the Halloween Symbols

Lilies, Rabbits, and Painted Eggs
The Story of the Easter Symbols

I'm Nobody! Who Are You?
The Story of Emily Dickinson

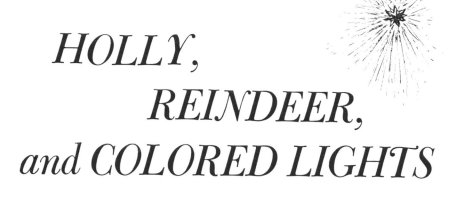

HOLLY, REINDEER, and COLORED LIGHTS

The Story of the Christmas Symbols

by EDNA BARTH

illustrated by

URSULA ARNDT

CLARION BOOKS
TICKNOR & FIELDS : A HOUGHTON MIFFLIN COMPANY
NEW YORK

Clarion Books
Ticknor & Fields, a Houghton Mifflin Company

Text copyright © 1971 by Edna Barth
Illustrations copyright © 1971 by Ursula Arndt
Library of Congress Catalog Card Number: 71-157731
ISBN 0-395-28842-8   Paperback ISBN 0-89919-037-5
(Previously published by The Seabury Press
under ISBN 0-8164-3023-3)

Designed by Carol Basen
Printed in the United States of America

P 15 14 13

Contents

*H*olly *and reindeer, angels and stars,* fire-places and chimneys, trees sparkling with colored lights. Many weeks before Christmas, these and other holiday symbols appear all around us—in our homes, schools, and stores, or as decorations for our streets. Some of them, like the angels, express the religious meaning of this Christian holiday. Others, like the reindeer, express the lighter side. All of them express joy.

Each holiday symbol has a story. Many of them take us back to the first Christmas or long before.

Christmas—and Before

Christmas celebrates the birth nearly two thousand years ago of Jesus Christ, who Christians believe was the son of God. The exact date of his birth is not known, but there were good reasons for choosing December 25 for the Christ's Mass, or feast day.

For hundreds of years before Christ, people had worshiped the sun. Those in the northern hemisphere noticed, with fear, a time of the year when the sun god seemed to forsake them. Each day was a little shorter than the one before. If this continued, there would be no light or life left on earth at all. But in the end, the god always relented, they discovered, for the days gradually became longer.

We now call this time of the shortest days, the winter *solstice*. The earth travels around the sun in a journey that takes a year. It travels tilted on the axis running from the North to the South Pole. About September 23, the North Pole begins tilting away from the sun. Each day, less direct sunlight reaches the northern hemisphere, and the noonday sun appears at

8

a lower point in the sky. Finally, around December 22, we have our shortest day and the beginning of winter. For several days the sun appears at the same low point—a solstice, a "standing still."

At this season people of northern Europe kindled lights and fires to help the sun god relight his lamp. They feasted and rejoiced, for now there would be another spring. Crops would grow, and life would flourish.

This was the season, too, when the Romans honored Saturn, god of agriculture, with their *Saturnalia* festival. It was a time for visiting friends, exchanging gifts, for feasting and dancing. Masked revelers filled the streets.

During the Jewish month of Kislev, which falls in December, the ancient Hebrews observed *Hanukkah,* the Festival of the Dedication, sometimes called the Feast of Lights. Still celebrated, it marks an early victory in the Jews' struggle to worship one god in their own way.

The Persians lighted fires at the winter solstice in praise of Mithra, god of light. The ancient Egyptians held a festival that honored Isis, mother of the sun god Horus.

All such midwinter festivals hailed the victory of light and life.

To the first Christians, the coming of Christ and his believed resurrection to life after death meant very much the same thing. Christ was "the light of the world."

Few in number, early Christians within the Roman Empire worshiped secretly for fear of punishment. Most Romans, including emperors, were still devoted to older, pagan gods. Gradually, more and more people became Christians. Then in the fourth century, by special edict, the Roman emperor Constantine I declared Christianity lawful.

Thousands of Romans, loyal to the old gods, still celebrated the Saturnalia. Thousands of others had begun worshiping the Persian Mithra. To them, December 25 was "The Birthday of the Unconquered Sun," the start of a new year.

When people like these gave up their pagan gods to worship the Christian god, they were encouraged to mark the rebirth of the year by thanking the father god who had sent them Christ. The sun had become "the son."

Within the church, Jesus' birthday was at first ignored. Since the true date was unknown, earlier Christians had celebrated it at various times. At last, in the year 350, Pope Julius I set the probable date as December 25.

10

Christians in most places accepted this, but there were some who disliked a date so closely linked with pagan holidays. The Armenians, for example, chose to observe Christmas on January 6, as they still do.

How and when Christmas is celebrated today and how long the holiday lasts varies from place to place. The Christmas season may start, as it does in the Netherlands, on December 6, St. Nicholas Day. It may extend, as it does in Mexico, Spain, or Puerto Rico, to Three Kings' Day on January 6, or even beyond.

In the United States, the most festive part of the season lasts, usually, from Christmas Eve to New Year's Day. But in a country composed of people from many parts of the world, Christmas customs are as rich in variety as the people themselves.

The Christmas Star

At the top of a Christmas tree, on a Christmas card, in the shape of a cookie, or outlined in brilliant lights, the star reappears each Christmas.

People of ancient times created myths about the stars, and sometimes regarded them as gods. Stars have guided sailors at night. They have inspired poets, musicians, and painters.

Long before the first Christmas, stars had an important place in other religions. The people of ancient Babylon, who wrote in word pictures, repeated the star symbol three times to mean a god. Ancient Egyptians believed that certain gods controlled the various stars. In China, the stars and constellations themselves were objects of worship. The ancient Hebrews took as their symbol the six-pointed star of David, which is still the emblem of the Jewish people. The Blackfoot Indians of North America believed that each star was at one time a human being. Today in North Africa some of the Berber tribes worship the con-

12

stellations of the Great Bear and Little Bear, as they have for centuries.

But the five-pointed star of Christmas is unique.

At the time of the birth of Jesus, the New Testament says, a strange star appeared over Bethlehem. Guided by its light, wise men came on camels from other kingdoms, to honor the event.

What was the star of Bethlehem, and where is it now? New stars, or *novas,* do appear every now and then. But though the exact date of Jesus' birth is unknown, astronomers say that no new star appeared in the sky anywhere near the probable time. Aside from novas, the same stars are in the sky today as were there nearly two thousand years ago.

Could the Christmas star have been one of the meteors we call shooting stars? No, say the astronomers. A light, feathery meteor appears in the earth's atmosphere for only a few seconds. The wise men were guided by their star for weeks.

Nor could the star of Bethlehem have been a comet, though comets are often brilliant enough to be seen with the naked eye for weeks or months. Modern astronomers know which comets were close to earth hundreds and thousands of years ago. There was no bright comet visible to human beings when Jesus was born.

Studies made by astronomers and historians, combined with clues found in the Bible, suggest that Jesus was born, not in the year 1 A.D., but in the springtime of 6 B.C. At that time the planets Mars, Jupiter, and Saturn were close together in the heavens. They formed a triangle in the group of stars known as *Pisces*.

The wise men were astrologers and studied the motions of the stars and planets. They knew, too, that, according to Jewish rabbis, Mars, Jupiter, and Saturn had appeared together in Pisces a few years before the birth of the Hebrew prophet Moses. Pisces was, therefore, the special constellation of the Jewish people. To the wise men, the grouping of the three planets in it may have been the sign of a great event in the land of the Jewish people. This may have been the star of Bethlehem.

Nevertheless, many people prefer to believe that the strange star did appear, and that it was simply a miracle.

In many parts of the world today, including Poland, Spain, Italy, Iran, and Russia,

celebration of the Christian holiday has usually begun with the appearance of the first star on Christmas Eve.

In Poland this signals the beginning of the Festival of the Star. After the Christmas Eve meal, the village priest, as the "Star Man," tests the children's religious knowledge. In parts of Alaska boys and girls carry a star figure from house to house, singing carols and hoping for treats. In Hungary a star-shaped pattern in an apple cut in half means good luck. A broken pattern foretells illness.

Throughout history, the star has been a symbol of high hopes and high ideals—hope for good fortune, hope for reaching above oneself.

To many Christians the Christmas star expresses the ideals held out by Jesus, called in the Bible "the bright and morning star."

For all human beings, regardless of religion, stars in general have special meaning. And all share the heavens, no matter what barriers keep them apart on earth.

The Christmas Tree

An evergreen tree, sparkling with ornaments and colored lights, topped sometimes with a star, means Christmas to many people today.

To human beings who lived long before there was a Christmas, a decorated tree had special meaning, too.

In what is now England and France there lived, several thousand years ago, a group of Celtic people known as *Druids*. Sorcerers, priests, prophets, and healers, they worshiped nature, practiced magic, and held secret ceremonies in sacred groves.

At the winter solstice, the Druid priests decorated oak trees with gilded apples and lighted candles. The apples expressed gratitude to the god Odin for bestowing fruits. The candles honored the sun god Balder.

At the Saturnalia in December the ancient Romans trimmed trees with trinkets and candles, placing an image of the sun god at the tip.

16

The Egyptian Isis was the goddess of growing things, as well as mother of the sun god Horus. At her festival in late December, palm branches were taken into Egyptian homes, as a symbol of continuing life.

According to a legend, the first Christmas tree was revealed by a miracle one Christmas Eve about twelve hundred years ago. Winfrid, the English missionary who was later named St. Boniface, was in Germany, trying to win over the pagan tribesmen. Finding a group of worshipers gathered at the Oak of Geismar, about to sacrifice little Prince Asulf to the god Thor, Winfrid stopped them. He cut down the "blood oak" before their eyes, and as it fell, a young fir tree sprang up. The fir tree was the tree of Christ, Winfrid said, a symbol of goodness and love that should be taken into their homes. Then he told the tribesmen about the birth of Jesus.

Some believe that the Christmas tree may have come from the Paradise Tree of the Middle Ages. A fir tree hung with red apples, it appeared in *Adam and Eve,* one of the European miracle plays about events of the Bible. By the fifteenth century people were erecting Paradise Trees in their own homes on December 24, the feast day of Adam and Eve.

Others believe that the Christmas tree began in the sixteenth century with Martin Luther, the German Protestant leader of church reform. On Christmas Eve, legend has it, Martin Luther was inspired by the beauty of tall evergreens against a starry sky. He cut a fir tree, took it home to his family, and placed lighted candles on its branches. The lights, he said, stood for the stars in the heavens above Bethlehem.

The first real record of a Christmas tree is in a German book dated 1604. By the nineteenth century it had spread throughout Germany, to Austria, Finland, Denmark, Norway, and Sweden. In most of Germany there were plenty of trees. In other places, people sometimes covered a wooden pyramid with evergreens, tinsel, and candles.

In England, meanwhile, there were no Christmas trees, but celebrations were lively. Pranks and wrongdoing were common. Under a "lord of Misrule," revelers sometimes took control of a town.

Then, in 1642, the Puritan government under Oliver Cromwell banned Christian celebrations as rowdy and pagan. People were to work as usual. Stores were to be kept open. Anyone caught lighting a Christmas candle or

eating a Christmas cake was punished. Town criers went around shouting, "No Christmas! No Christmas!"

In 1660, with King Charles II on the throne, the Christmas holiday in England was revived. Two hundred years later the first Christmas tree appeared. Prince Albert, Queen Victoria's German husband, celebrated the birth of their first son in 1841 with a Christmas tree at Windsor Castle.

The whole court was delighted and soon followed his example. Before long the custom had spread throughout England, and to many parts of the British Empire.

The Christmas tree had already crossed the Atlantic with Hessian soldiers hired by the British to fight the colonists during the American Revolution. Homesick for their German Christmas, the Hessians set up Christmas trees in America as they had at home.

In colonies settled by Puritans, Christmas was not a holiday at the time of the Revolution. A Massachusetts law of 1659 had fined anyone found celebrating it. And though the law had since been repealed, disapproval lingered on.

By the nineteenth century, however, people from the European continent were pouring into the United States. With them they brought their Christmas customs, including the tree. Before long, one state after another made Christmas a legal holiday.

Among the evergreens used for Christmas, the fir tree reigns supreme. In one of the many fir tree legends, a cold, hungry child knocked at a poor forester's door one Christmas Eve and was welcomed. On Christmas morning, the family knew by the dazzling light around him that he was the Christ Child. In reward for their kindness the Christ Child planted before their door a tiny fir tree that, at Christmas, would bear fruit.

Today, fir, spruce, and pine are the most popular Christmas trees. Some are grown on tree plantations. Some come from American or Canadian forests. Many people oppose cutting them. Others claim that cutting small trees permits fuller growth to larger, stronger trees.

Millions of American families now decorate fireproof artificial Christmas trees. Still others buy living trees. After Christmas, if they have a yard or garden, they plant them there. City people sometimes give them to a park.

"The Children's Christmas Tree," a tall spruce, grows in Independence Square in Philadelphia. Carols are sung around it on Christmas Eve.

Each Christmas the President of the United States lights a tall spruce on the White House lawn. It is decorated with large colored balls, one for each state.

The town of Wilmington, North Carolina, decks an ancient oak tree with 7,000 lights and six tons of Spanish moss. "The Nation's Christmas Tree" stands in King's Canyon National Park in California. It is a giant sequoia, over 3,500 years old.

In New Zealand, a tree shaped something like a Japanese bonsai blooms with red flowers in December or January and is called the Christmas Tree.

Africans of Liberia who celebrate Christmas cut oil palms, and decorate them with red bells.

Christmas Tree Ornaments

Fruits, gilded nuts, gingerbread, paper roses, the Christ Child with the wings of an angel. These were the decorations on the first Christmas trees in Germany. Later, glass balls in beautiful colors replaced the fruits. Then German ornament makers began shipping their wares to other countries, including the United States.

In American homes before then, ornaments had been homemade. Children enjoyed making long strings of popcorn and cranberries, paper chains, and paper stars. Sometimes they cut and colored a St. Nicholas figure. Their mother added apples, oranges, nuts, and popcorn balls.

Today most American Christmas trees are loaded with ornaments and colored lights bought at a store—dazzling balls, bells, and stars, elves, reindeer, and angels, tiny stockings and horns, sparkling tinsel, and gleaming icicles—symbols from many ages and many lands.

Horns and bells were once used to scare off evil spirits. Early Christmas trees had, in place of angels, figures of fairies—the good spirits.

On Polish Christmas trees, as well as many stars, there are always angels, peacocks and other birds. Swedish people hang gaily painted wooden ornaments, and straw figures of animals and children. In Denmark there are mobiles of bells, stars, snowflakes, and hearts, and sometimes strings of tiny Danish flags. Japanese Christians often adorn their trees with tiny fans and paper lanterns.

Lithuanian women make straw bird cages, stars, and geometric shapes, the straw expressing a wish for good crops in the coming year.

Czechoslovakian trees are hung with ornaments made of painted egg shells.

A Ukrainian Christmas tree has a spider and web for good luck. The symbol sprang from a legend of a poor woman with nothing to put on her children's tree. On Christmas morning she woke to find the branches covered with spider webs turned to silver by the rising sun.

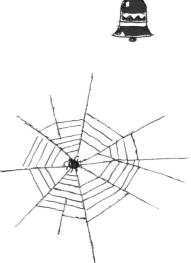

Christmas Greens and Flowers

As Christmas approaches, wreaths and garlands of pine, holly, mistletoe, and other evergreens appear on front doors, in classrooms, offices, stores, and churches, in magazine pictures and on Christmas cards.

Long before there was a Christmas, primitive tribes in Europe hung evergreens above their doors at this time of the year. During winter, they believed, the woodland spirits were forced to wander around in the cold. By offering them shelter within their homes, they hoped for good fortune and good health.

The ancient Romans decked their homes with evergreens at the Saturnalia festival and at the Kalends of January, their New Year. Friends gave one another green branches for good luck.

To the Druids, "the plants that do not die" were sacred, a symbol of life itself.

24

MISTLETOE

To kiss someone or to be kissed oneself under a bunch of mistletoe is often a part of the Christmas fun.

How did this aerial parasite, with its waxy white berries and leathery evergreen leaves, enter Christmas? Why is it hung high? Why always overhead? And why the kissing?

Among the Norsemen, mistletoe was sacred to Frigga, goddess of love and mother of the sun god Balder. Norse myth describes how Balder alarmed his mother by dreaming of death. Should the sun god die, all life on earth would end.

Frigga went at once to air, fire, water, earth, and every animal and plant. From each of these she drew a promise not to harm her son. One lowly plant she overlooked—the mistletoe, a parasite on oak and apple trees.

The cunning Loki, god of evil, was jealous of Balder, and saw here a chance to destroy his enemy, who stood for goodness as well as for sun and light. Making an arrowtip of the mistletoe, Loki gave it to Hoder, the blind god of winter, who shot it, striking Balder.

The god of light was dead!

The sky paled, and all the gods mourned.

For three days each one in turn tried to bring Balder back to life. With the power of love, Frigga succeeded.

The tears she had shed for her son turned into berries on the mistletoe plant. In her joy, Frigga kissed each one who passed beneath the tree on which it grew. Never again, Frigga decreed, should humble mistletoe do harm. Anyone standing under it would receive a token of love—a kiss.

Among the Druid sun worshipers, the sacred mistletoe was never allowed to touch the ground.

In late winter, when the branches of the oaks were bare, tiny yellow flowers appeared on the mistletoe. Surely this meant that the sun drew its golden light from the plant. In the mistletoe, then, lay the life of their sacred oak. The missel thrush had brought it from heaven, the Druids believed, to feed on its berries and carry its seeds from tree to tree.

At the Druids' winter solstice ceremony, the high priest mounted an oak tree. Using a golden sickle, he cut off the sacred mistletoe.

Those waiting below caught it in the folds of their robes. The high priest blessed sprigs of mistletoe, giving them out, and expecting gifts in return.

Followers wore the mistletoe, or hung it above their doorways to ward off evil spirits. All who entered received a kiss of friendship.

The ancient Greeks, too, believed that mistletoe could ward off evil. The Romans knew it as the "golden bough" of Aeneas, hero of Virgil's *Aeneid*. On his winter visit to the underworld, Aeneas took the plant as a gift to Persephone, goddess of seasons.

Long after Christianity replaced many older religions, faith in mistletoe lived on. Forbidden in churches as pagan, it became a part of Christmas in people's homes.

It was thought to bring about a happy marriage, ensure that a couple would have children, and cure sickness. To keep their herds healthy, farmers fed mistletoe to cows who bore calves during the holidays. Sprigs of mistletoe were hung over stable doors.

Today mistletoe is a symbol of Christmas joy. To let it fall to the ground is unlucky, people say, just as the Druids did so long ago. A girl standing under it cannot refuse to be kissed. One who goes unkissed cannot expect to be married the following year. Superstitions like these, whether believed or not, add to the fun at Christmas parties.

27

HOLLY

The Druids believed that holly, with its glossy leaves and red berries, remained green so the world would remain beautiful when the sacred oak had lost its leaves. Going into the forest to watch their priests cut the sacred mistletoe, the Druids wore sprigs of holly in their hair.

The plant was sacred to Saturn, the god honored at the Roman Saturnalia festival. The Romans gave one another holly wreaths, carried it in processions, and decked images of Saturn with it.

For several centuries after Christ, most of the Roman Empire went on worshiping the older, pagan gods. Cruel punishment could befall those worshiping Christ. In December, while other Romans celebrated the Saturnalia, the Christians celebrated the birth of Jesus. To avoid notice, they decked their homes with Saturnalia holly.

As the Christians grew in number and their customs prevailed, holly, once sacred to a pagan god, became a symbol of Christmas.

Then in 575 Bishop Martin of Bracae in Germany forbade all Christmas evergreens as

28

a dangerous heathen custom. It was several hundred years before they were seen again in churches.

By the seventeenth century, holly had once more become a part of Christmas merriment, and William Shakespeare had written these lines:

   Then, heigh ho, the holly!
This life is most jolly.

There are two kinds of holly, one prickly and one smooth. In a European household with prickly holly at Christmas, it was thought that the husband would rule during the coming year. Smooth holly meant wife-rule.

British farmers put sprigs of holly on their beehives. On the first Christmas, they believed, the bees hummed in honor of the Christ Child.

Because the plant had come to stand for peace and joy, people often settled quarrels beneath a holly tree. Planted near a home, it was said to frighten off witches, and protect the dwelling from thunder and lightning. A sprig of holly on the bedpost brought happy dreams. A tonic made from holly could cure a cough.

IVY

Like holly and mistletoe, ivy, another evergreen, had been a symbol of eternal life in pagan religions. In the Christian religion, it came to stand for the new promise of eternal life.

Although ivy is not a Christmas evergreen in the United States, it is still a favorite in England. Through the centuries English people have come to think of the sturdy holly as masculine, and clinging ivy as feminine.

LAUREL

In ancient Rome, the first Christians decorated their homes at the Saturnalia with laurel, or bay, as well as holly. Among the Romans who remained pagan, laurel was sacred to the sun god Apollo. As more and more people became Christians, laurel became a symbol of Christmas.

ROSEMARY

Rosemary, an evergreen now used to season foods, was once a Christmas plant. During the Middle Ages housewives spread it on the floor at Christmas. As people walked on it, a pleasant aroma arose. According to tradition, the shrub is fragrant because Mary laid the garments of the Christ Child on its branches. The night he was born, other legends say, trees suddenly bore fruit and flowers blossomed out of season.

THE POINSETTIA

Legends like those above helped keep alive a love of special Christmas plants and flowers. A favorite in the United States is the poinsettia, with its red, star-shaped flower. Known in Central America as Flame Leaf or Flower of the Holy Night, it was brought here over a hundred years ago by Dr. Joel Poinsett, our first ambassador to Mexico.

A Mexican legend tells of a poor girl who, with no gift to offer Mary, picked some flowering weeds along the roadside. The moment she placed them before the Virgin's statue, they turned into brilliant poinsettia blossoms.

In the Poinsettia Belt of California, growers pot and ship these Christmas plants to every state in the Union.

THE CHRISTMAS ROSE

Until the twentieth century, the Christmas rose was grown in England as the poinsettia is grown here. A true Christmas flower, native to the mountains of Central Europe, it blooms in the depths of winter.

Legends link it with the birth of Christ. In one, the wise men and the shepherds, traveling together, passed a field where little Madelon was tending her sheep. At the sight of their gifts for the Christ Child, the young shepherdess began to weep. Even the shepherds had something to offer—fruits, honey, and a white dove. Madelon had nothing, not even a simple flower. An angel, seeing her weeping, brushed the snow away, revealing a lovely white flower tipped with pink—the Christmas rose.

Candles and Colored Lights

Every Christmas, glowing candles appear in windows, on fireplace mantels and dinner tables, in the hands of carolers, and on greeting cards, wrappings, and ribbons.

Lighted candles are symbols, not only of Christmas, but of Easter and birthdays, too. Some form of light has marked all man's occasions of joy.

Centuries before the birth of Jesus, people lighted torches as well as bonfires at their winter solstice rites. The ancient Scandinavians built fires to defy the Frost King. The Persians kindled them in honor of Mithra, god of light. At the Saturnalia the Romans put lighted candles on small trees in honor of Saturn, who ruled their crops. The Druids lighted them for the sun god Balder.

At Hanukkah, Jewish people have, for centuries, lighted candles in a *Menorah*, one more each evening until eight plus a *shamash*, or servant candle, are all burning. The first Hanukkah, in 165 B.C., marked a glorious victory for religious freedom. The Jews had just defeated an invading monarch with his alien gods. Now they rededicated the Temple at Jerusalem.

In a legend that arose later, they found enough pure oil to keep the Eternal Lamp burning just one day, but, by a miracle, it burned for eight.

For all ancient peoples, new light meant new life.

People of the Middle Ages put lighted candles in their windows on Christmas Eve to guide the Christ Child on his way. No stranger was turned away. For—who knew—he might be the Christ Child in disguise.

Farmers led their horses and cattle into the barn on Christmas Eve, holding candles to light the way. Some went to their stables with tapers to bless the animals.

One huge candle was often set aflame on Christmas Eve. If it went out before the end of Christmas Day, that meant bad luck for the coming year. In Denmark there were usually

34

two such candles, one for the master of the house and one for the mistress.

Today people of the Russian or Greek Orthodox religion light candles on the night of January 5, their Christmas Eve.

Children in Labrador receive candles stuck in turnips. Made of deer tallow at one time, the candles were eaten. Today the children eat only the turnip.

Filipino children put candles in colored lanterns and march in parade.

In Spain each family places a burning candle above the door on Christmas Eve. In Italy candles shine in the windows of homes to light the way for the Holy Child.

In New Guinea, on each of the four Sundays before Christmas, a candle inserted in a slanting board symbolizes the *Advent,* or coming of Christ. On Christmas a larger candle placed at the high end proclaims his birth.

In many English, German, and American homes an Advent wreath with four candles in

it is placed in the window, on a table, or hung from the ceiling. One candle is lighted on each of the four Sundays before Christmas, until all are burning.

Throughout the United States, there are Christmas candlelight services. The Central Moravian church in Pennsylvania has an especially beautiful one. It was first held in 1741 when Count Nicholas von Zinzendorf, holding one lighted candle, led a band of people into a cabin in southeastern Pennsylvania and named their settlement Bethlehem. Today each person receives a lighted candle at the end of the church service on Christmas Eve.

Before modern electricity, candles also decorated Christmas trees. Now trees are usually strung with colored lights, and sometimes they decorate whole houses or whole streets. On rooftops and front lawns there are lighted tableaux of Christmas figures from Santa and reindeer to the entire manger scene. The American Christmas is a feast of lights.

In some Italian towns, in Mexico, the Philippine Islands, and sometimes in the southern United States, firecrackers or fireworks go off on Christmas Eve or Christmas Day.

36

There are even places where the holiday is greeted with cannons or guns—around Berchtesgaden, Germany, for one. A Christmas custom now, the loud noise was once thought to awaken sleeping spirits of the forests and fields.

On Christmas Eve in Iraq, there is a still earlier form of fire. Iraqi Christians gather in their courtyards around bonfires made of thorns. If all the thorns turn to ashes, it means good luck. Each person jumps over the ashes and makes a wish.

Outside Mexican-American homes in New Mexico, too, small bonfires blaze on Christmas Eve.

A flickering candle, a display of lights, a bonfire, an exploding firecracker or booming gun—all express Christmas joy, a joy in warmth, light, and life itself.

The Yule Log

When fires blazed in open hearths in every home, no Christmas was complete without a Yule log. Brought in with great ceremony on Christmas Eve, it was kindled from the charred remains of the last year's log.

Today the Yule log is still a symbol of Christmas. We find it on Christmas cards, as the centerpiece of a dinner table, in log-shaped cakes or even ice cream.

Like so many Christmas symbols, it has a story that goes far back in history.

To the Norsemen of Europe, the sun was *hweol,* a wheel of fire rolling toward them for a time, and then away. Each winter when the sun wheel began to turn toward earth again, they rejoiced. The powers of darkness had failed to overcome the god of light!

Animals were slaughtered for feasting. Huge bonfires blazed.

From the Norse name for the turning time of the sun, *Hweolor-tid,* came the word yuletide. Like *Natale,* the Italian name for Christmas, and like the French *Noel,* it once meant the beginning of a new year.

38

The Druids, who set lighted candles on tree branches and cut mistletoe at the winter solstice, burned a Yule log as well. This was always the trunk of a stout oak or apple tree. They blessed the log, praying that it would burn forever. Each year they saved a brand from the Yuletide fire to kindle the next one.

Early tribes of Scandinavia worshiped *Yggdrasil,* Tree of the Universe. One root of the tree lay in heaven, one in hell, and one on earth. Gnawing at the roots were evil serpents who might, one day, destroy the universe.

In time these northern tribes became Christian. Though Christmas replaced their winter solstice festival, they went on believing in Yggdrasil. Finally the church persuaded them to burn a Yule log which would stand for their mystic tree. "Now," the church fathers explained, "the Tree of the Universe is gone, and with it your pagan beliefs."

From Scandinavia the Yule log custom spread through the European continent and to England. Months before Christmas a tree was chosen, cut down, and allowed to dry. Some logs were so huge that horses or oxen were harnessed to haul them home. Usually the family did the hauling. All who helped would be safe from witchcraft, so everyone, young or old, usually lent a hand.

Some families decked their Yule log with greenery, ribbons, and paper flowers, singing Yuletide songs as they dragged it home. Seeing such a procession, a passer-by would remove his hat.

Indoors, there were songs and ceremonies of all sorts. The head of the family or the very youngest might pour wine over the log. And there was always a prayer for happiness, health, and wealth. Sometimes each person present sat on the log and made a wish. Finally the log was set ablaze.

Past quarrels forgotten, a family drew together. The burning Yule log drove out evil spirits, they believed. By beating it with a stick, they could see them leave in a shower of sparks. Sometimes children were told to do this, and to ask forgiveness for their sins.

On no account must the Yule log be entirely burned. As an old English ditty warned:

> Part must be kept wherewith to tende
> The Christmas log next yeare,
> And where 'tis safely kept, the fiend
> Can do no mischiefe theere.

In some vicinities only a person with freshly washed hands could touch the log. While it burned, if a barefooted person or one who squinted arrived, bad luck was close by. A log that stopped burning during the night meant bad luck for the entire year.

In the Balkan countries and other parts of Europe, farmers put Yule log ashes in the clefts of fruit trees to improve the crop. In many homes the master put the ashes under the bed to keep lightning from striking the house.

English settlers brought the Yule log custom to what is now the southern United States. There, Christmas Eve merrymaking went on as long as the log burned. Dancing ended with the Virginia reel, and by that time it was usually dawn.

Fireplaces and chimneys, like the Yule log, are symbols from a time when Christmas itself was unknown.

To the cave man, a blazing fire that kept wild beasts away at night meant safety as well as warmth.

At the winter solstice, the early Germans welcomed Hertha, goddess of the home. Surrounded by their serfs, a wealthy family would gather for a feast in their great hall. Evergreens decked the walls. Near the table was an altar of flat stones heaped high with fir boughs.

The boughs were set afire. Then—it was believed—Hertha descended through the smoke, bestowing good fortune on all.

The flat stones of Hertha's altar became the hearthstones of later houses. The fireplace and chimney became symbols of safety and home. Hertha herself was an ancestor of later gift bringers.

Santa Claus and His Ancestors

Santa Claus is only one of many Christmas gift bringers, and was not always the jolly fat man in a red suit we know today.

Thousands of years before Christ, the Scandinavian god Odin rode through the world at midwinter on his eight-footed horse Sleipnir, bringing reward or punishment.

His son Thor, god of farming, thunder, and war, made his home in the far North. His weapon was lightning, his color red. At midwinter he fought the gods of ice and snow, and conquered the cold.

At the same season, the gentle German goddess Hertha descended with her gifts of good fortune and health.

The Christian religion brought the end of such pagan gods, in form at least. Later, as St. Nicholas and Father Christmas, they reappeared in spirit.

Born in Asia Minor in the fourth century, the boy Nicholas grew up to become a bishop. Legends tell of his kindness, his love for children, and of miracles he brought about. On an ocean voyage to the Holy Land, he was said to have quelled a tempest, and restored life to a dying sailor. He was also said to have brought three murdered schoolboys back to life with love and prayers.

A certain nobleman with three daughters and no dowries for them had nowhere to turn. When the first daughter was ready to marry, the good bishop Nicholas tossed a bag of gold into the house at night. Later the second daughter also received a mysterious bag of gold. When the third daughter's turn came, the nobleman kept watch and saw the bishop toss another bag of gold into the house. The bishop begged the girl's father not to tell, but the news got out.

The third bag of gold, it was said, fell into a stocking hung by the chimney to dry. This, some believe, is the reason we hang up Christmas stockings.

Stories of the bishop's generosity spread. Anyone who received an unexpected gift thanked Nicholas.

Six hundred years after Bishop Nicholas'

44

death, the Russian Emperor Vladimir visited Constantinople. There, hearing all the wonderful stories, he decided to make Nicholas the patron saint of Russia. In time, word of the kind bishop passed through northern Siberia into Lapland—to the people of the reindeer sleds.

Statues and pictures show the saint with three bags of gold. Merchants of northern Italy took him for their patron, placing three gilded balls before their doors. Since the merchants lent money at times, the golden balls became the symbol of pawnbrokers.

St. Nicholas is the patron of a number of cities in Europe. In Greece, many boys are still named for him. And there is hardly a seacoast in any Catholic country without a chapel dedicated to him. For Nicholas is the patron saint of sailors, as well as of children.

The anniversary of his death, December 6, came so close to Christmas that, in many countries, the two merged. In Germany and the Netherlands, however, St. Nicholas Day remained apart.

Dutch children were told that St. Nicholas, or *Sinterklaas,* sailed from Spain with a Moorish helper. They filled their shoes with hay and sugar for his horse and woke up to find

45

them filled with nuts and candies. In homes where Sinterklaas appeared in his bishop's robes in person, he usually resembled the father or oldest son, and knew a great deal about the children's behavior. At that time, St. Nicholas carried a birch rod as well as presents, in case the children had misbehaved. Today he is more kindly.

Children in old Czechoslovakia believed that *Svaty Mikulas* was brought down from heaven on a golden cord by an angel. When Svaty Mikulas arrived on Christmas, the children rushed to the table to say their prayers. If they did well, he told the angel who came with him to give them their presents.

In parts of the Alps, "ghosts of the field" cleared the way for St. Nicholas. Behind them came a man wearing a goat's head, and a masked demon with a birch switch.

In the Berchtesgaden district of Germany, twelve young men dressed in straw and wearing animal masks danced along after St. Nicholas, ringing cowbells. At each house, after gifts were given, the masked men drove the

young people out and beat them, or pretended to. A symbolic punishment for idleness or misbehavior, it was once part of a pagan ritual to ensure crops.

At the prow of the ship in which the Dutch sailed to the New World in 1630 was a figure of St. Nicholas. He wore a broad-brimmed hat and held a long-stemmed Dutch pipe.

The writer Washington Irving described him in 1809 as a chubby little man with a jolly smile, drawn by a team of reindeer.

This portrait so delighted Dr. Clement Moore of New York City that he wrote "A Visit from St. Nicholas," the poem that begins:

'Twas the night before Christmas
    when all through the house
Not a creature was stirring, not even
    a mouse;

A family friend heard Dr. Moore read the poem to his children, and copied it down. The next Christmas she sent it to a newspaper, the *Sentinel* in Troy, New York. It appeared in December, 1823, without the author's name.

All who read it were delighted with St. Nicholas as Dr. Moore saw him:

He had a broad face and little round
　　belly,
That shook when he laughed like a
　　bowlful of jelly.

Dr. Moore, himself a professor of Divinity, felt it beneath his dignity to admit that he had written the poem. It was many years before he did.

Read and loved by children and grownups alike each Christmas, the poem won still more friends for the new, jollier St. Nicholas.

Thomas Nast, who drew a series of Christmas cartoons for *Harper's Weekly*, remembered the *Pelznickel*, or Furry Nicholas, of his childhood in Bavaria. In a famous cartoon of

1866 he showed Santa in his workshop with his record of the good and bad deeds of all children. In the picture were the sleigh and reindeer, stockings hung by the fireplace, and the Christmas tree. The red-faced, roly-poly little man had become the Santa Claus Americans know today.

Back in the sixteenth century, Martin Luther had declared that St. Nicholas was robbing Christmas of its true meaning. As a result, in much of Germany, and in parts of Switzerland, the Christ Child, *Christkind,* became the gift giver.

The gifts of the Christ Child are brought by his messenger, a young girl with a golden crown who holds a tiny "Tree of Light."

Swedish children wait eagerly for *Jultomten,* a gnome whose sleigh is drawn by the

Julbocker, the goats of the thunder god Thor. With his red suit and cap, and a bulging sack on his back, he looks much like the American Santa Claus.

In Denmark, too, the gift bringer *Julemanden* carries a sack and is drawn by reindeer. Elves known as *Juul Nisse* are said to come from the attic, where they live, to help with the chores during Yuletide. The children put a saucer of milk or rice pudding for them in the attic. In the morning they are delighted to find it empty.

In Poland the children's gifts are said to come from the stars, while in Hungary the angels bring them. Children of Syria receive theirs from the Youngest Camel on January 6, which is Three Kings' Day.

Children of Spain, Mexico, Puerto Rico, the Philippines, and such South American countries as Argentina and Brazil, also receive their gifts at this time, but from the Three Kings themselves.

Italian children, too, are given gifts on

Three Kings' Day, but the gift bringer is *La Befana,* the same ageless wanderer known in Russia as *Baboushka.*

La Befana refused to go to Bethlehem with the wise men when they passed her door. The Russian Baboushka misdirected them. Both women have searched for the Christ Child ever since. On the eve of Three Kings' Day they wander from house to house, peering into the faces of children and leaving gifts.

English children wait for Father Christmas, known to their ancestors as Christmas itself. Driven underground by the Puritan ban on celebrations, the gray-bearded old gentleman reappeared during Queen Victoria's reign. In time he acquired reindeer and sleigh, a sack of toys, and a home at the North Pole.

To Christians in the African Republic of Ghana, Father Christmas comes from the jungle. In Hawaii he comes by boat. On the Nerang River in Australia he rides on water skis, sporting a white beard and red bathing trunks.

Father Christmas, La Befana, the Three Kings, Santa Claus, the elves, the gnomes, and the many others all express the desire people feel at Christmas to share, to give, to show love —especially love of children.

51

Christmas Gifts

Gift giving at the time we now celebrate Christmas began long ago. At the Roman Saturnalia, rich men gave fairly generously to the poor. The poor, in return, gave tapers, frankincense, and garlands of holly or laurel. Children were given little images made of clay or paste.

At the Kalends of January, the Roman New Year, people gave one another *strenae*. At first these were green boughs from the grove of the goddess Strenia. Later there were gifts that served as charms—"honeyed things" for sweetness in the coming year, lamps for light and warmth, silver and gold objects to ensure wealth.

If the first Christians gave one another gifts at Christmas it was not with the blessing of the church. Gifts had been too much a part of pagan holidays. But by the twelfth century, in many parts of Europe people were exchanging gifts. In Catholic countries such as France, Spain, Italy, and throughout Latin America, Christmas Day is still usually a holy day, with gifts given on another day.

52

In the Middle Ages, children's gifts often came in bundles of three. There was something rewarding, something useful, and something for discipline.

English monarchs demanded Christmas gifts from their subjects. This was one of the ways in which Queen Elizabeth I replenished her wardrobe. Nobles, clergymen, cooks, bakers, and all the palace servants gave, each according to his rank and means. The Queen received rich furs and jewels, handsome petticoats, and, once, the first pair of silk stockings to appear in Europe.

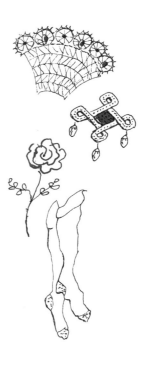

Slaves on some of the southern plantations in the United States had a custom called "Christmas Gif'." When two of them met on Christmas Day, each would try to be the first to cry out "Christmas Gif'." The loser gave the winner a few nuts or a Christmas cupcake. From the slave cabins the custom spread to the "Big House," becoming a Christmas tradition of the Old South.

Today, in Colombia the same sort of game is called *aguinaldo,* a word meaning Christmas gift.

53

In a religious sense, a Christmas gift is a symbol of the gifts taken to Bethlehem by the wise men, also known as the Magi or Three Kings. In the words of the Bible, ". . . they saw the young child with Mary his mother, and fell down, and worshiped him; and when they had opened their treasures, they presented unto him gifts; gold, and frankincense, and myrrh."

Each gift foretold something Christ would become—gold, a king; frankincense, a high priest; myrrh, a healer and a martyr.

The Christmas Manger

In the Middle Ages, when few people could read and church services were all in Latin, other ways were found of teaching the Bible stories. A group of carved figures showing the baby Jesus, Mary and Joseph, the shepherds, the kings, and the animals of the stable was one means of telling the story of Jesus' birth, the nativity.

To St. Francis of Assisi, the founder of the Franciscan order of friars, this was not enough. In 1224, in a cave outside the Italian town of Greccio, he set up a manger scene with real animals and live people. The Christ Child, though life-size, was made of wax.

On Christmas Eve, from the countryside all around, farmers and shepherds brought their families to marvel at the sight. St. Francis told them to put hatred from their hearts, and make Christmas a time of peace and goodwill. Then he led them in what may have been the first Christmas carols. He urged the children to gather around the manger as they sang.

People slipped bits of the manger straw into their pockets. Surely, they thought, straw of this kind would have the power to cure sick farm animals.

St. Francis had given new life to the *presepe,* as the manger scene is called in Italian. The same ceremony was repeated every year thereafter, and was copied in other towns in Italy. Then people began setting up manger scenes in their homes. From Italy the idea spread to Spain, France, and Portugal.

As time went on, the Italian presepe grew more elaborate. The rich used costly statues by famous sculptors, adding more and more figures. The Italian countryside formed the setting.

Some of these presepes are now in the world's museums. One of the most famous is in the Basilica of Saints Cosmas and Damian in Rome.

It contains hundreds of wooden figurines, and measures forty-five by twenty feet. Done by famous seventeenth century artists of Naples, it shows what life was like around that city.

A Spanish manger scene, the *nacimiento,* always showed women washing clothes at a little stream. On a nearby hillside stood a Spanish bull. Spanish children sang and danced around the nacimiento to the music of the tambourine.

The nativity scene became the center of Christmas celebrations in southern Europe, just as the Christmas tree had in the north.

But German children of the Middle Ages had both a Christmas tree and a Christmas *Krippe,* as they called the nativity scene. The children sang and danced around the Krippe with such gusto that it often bounced. The church frowned on this "cradle rocking," but from it came a number of lovely Christmas lullabies.

From European countries the Christmas crib spread to England, but was never as popular there.

Today in Italy people shop for presepe figures just as Americans shop for tree ornaments. Even the poorest home has a presepe, with cardboard or plaster figures.

Children of France gather moss, stones, and greens for the nativity scene. In their country it is called the *creche*. Every evening until January 6, the children gather around it to sing.

In Latin America, families set up their manger scenes in mid-December. Where Spanish is spoken, they are called *nacimientos, pesebres,* or *portales.* People of Haiti use the French word *creche*.

In the wealthier South American homes, the figures may be works of art, brought from Spain and handed down in the family. Sometimes the scene occupies a whole room. Viewers look in at the door.

The actual manger is often kept empty until midnight of Christmas Eve when the infant Jesus is "born." It is usually left up until Three Kings' Day on January 6.

In nativity scenes, as in paintings, people have usually pictured the Christ Child and his attendants in their own image. Most Italian or Spanish figures have dark eyes and dark hair. In England or Germany, they are often blue-eyed and usually fair. African and Oriental Christians have shown the various members with African or Oriental features. Costumes, architecture, and the physical settings vary, too, and this is only natural. For people can understand and identify with things most easily when they are familiar.

The Three Kings

The Three Kings, or wise men, appear in paintings by such artists as Botticelli and Rubens as well as on the cheapest Christmas cards. In their splendid robes, with their camels, they appear every year in Christmas plays and pageants. They inspired Gian Carlo Menotti to write his opera *Amahl and the Night Visitor,* shown every year on American and British television.

The Three Kings were not really kings at all, and no one knows whether there were three or more. The Bible calls them simply "wise men from the East." The number three may have come from their three gifts—gold, frankincense, and myrrh.

The magi, as the "kings" are also called, were priests among the ancient Medes and Persians. Learned men and astrologers, they were known for their enchantments. No ruler took an important step without consulting them. From their name comes our word magic.

As early as the sixth century they were spoken of as kings. The English scholar Bede and others named them. One was Melchior,

60

they decided, ruler of Nubia and Arabia. Kaspar was king of Tarsus, a city in southern Turkey. Balthasar, a black man, ruled Ethiopia. It was not until the eleventh century, however, that they were shown with crowns.

The Three Kings came to stand for the three stages of life. In paintings, tableaux, or pageants, Melchior appears as a long-bearded old man, Balthasar is middle-aged, Kaspar a man of twenty.

Around their journey to Bethlehem, hundreds of legends arose. According to one, though they traveled for two years, their food and drink never gave out. In another, they traveled for twelve days that seemed like one, with no need to eat or rest. Back in their own kingdoms, they gave their wealth to the poor, going about themselves as humble preachers. Finally, in India, they died as martyrs.

Three hundred years later, legend goes on, their bodies were taken to Constantinople, from there to Italy, and later still to Cologne Cathedral in Germany.

There, skulls known as the Three Kings of Cologne may be seen today. Anything that had touched the skulls was once believed to prevent accidents. The kings' names were engraved on rings as a charm against illness.

61

The Christian church's name for Three Kings' Day, January 6, is *Epiphany,* meaning manifestation. According to church doctrine, on that day it was manifested to the kings that the baby born in the manger was sent by God.

When Christianity became the state religion in ancient Rome, the days between December 25 and January 6, the Kalends or New Year, became Twelve Holy Days, the last known as Twelfth Day. Germanic people reckoned by nights rather than days. When they became Christians, they called the period Twelve Holy Nights. Epiphany became Twelfth Night.

In Germany and Austria it was long the custom for boys to go about in fours on Twelfth Night. One carried a star at the end of a pole. The other three were dressed as kings.

In English churches the shepherds are removed from the manger scene on Twelfth Night and the wise men put in. At the royal chapel gold, frankincense, and myrrh are offered in the name of the Crown. In some of the homes, the wise men are put in place before Christmas, but as far as possible from the manger. Each day until Twelfth Night they are brought a little closer.

62

In Spain, where children receive their presents on Three Kings' Day, there is a special custom in some cities. Carrying cake for the kings, figs for the servants, and hay for the camels, the children troop out to the city gates, hoping to see the Three Kings in silhouette above the mountains.

Among others who receive their presents on Three Kings' Day are Filipino and Puerto Rican children. On January 12, which is Bethlehem Day in Puerto Rico, children march through the streets in parade, led by three kings on horses or ponies.

Until a century ago, Dutch, German, and English families had a special "Twelfth" cake. In France it was the Cake of the Kings. On its top there were stars, crowns, flowers, dragons, and little kings. Baked inside was a bean or pea. The person finding it was king or queen. In Quebec, Canada, where old French customs persist, many people still bake the Cake of the Kings.

The "wise men from the east," transformed into kings, have ridden their camels through hundreds of Christmases. They are symbols of reverence, of loving, and of giving.

63

The Angels' Message

Angels with trumpets are a favorite design for Christmas cards. "Hark the Herald Angels Sing" is a favorite carol. Made of spun glass or of shining metal, angels adorn many Christmas trees. Sometimes a single angel appears at the top. With the holy family, the wise men, and shepherds, angels appear in Christmas nativity scenes and in countless pageants.

Bodiless, immortal spirits, angels have a place in the traditional Jewish and Mohammedan religions as well as in Christianity.

64

Throughout the Bible angels appear at important moments, sometimes as protective guardians but more often as messengers from God. The New Testament tells how the "angel of the Lord" appeared to the "shepherds keeping watch over their flocks by night" to bring them "good tidings of great joy"—the birth of Jesus Christ. Then a multitude of angels proclaimed:

> Glory to God in the highest,
> and on earth peace,
> good will toward men.

Thousands of years before the first Christmas, at the same time of year, the Norsemen had a season of peace. Norse myths describe the gods' alarm when the sun god was struck dead. They would, at once, have slain his enemy, the god of winter and darkness, had it not occurred during their *peacestead*.

The ancient Romans had a similar custom. While the god Saturn reigned, they believed, the world had enjoyed a Golden Age of equality and peace. During the Saturnalia festival, farmers' disputes over water or cattle were put aside. War was outlawed. Peace and goodwill prevailed.

Today, in the spirit of the Christmas angels and ancient tradition, the holiday season is a time of forgiving, of making peace, of reaching out to others with goodwill. Prisoners are often pardoned at this season. Countries at war sometimes declare a holiday truce.

In Norway, an old maxim says that no door shall be locked, no quarrel left unsettled, and no mouse killed during the Christmas season.

Before the Christmas Eve feast in Poland, everyone at the table receives a peace wafer, a symbol of closeness and goodwill. Ukrainian people, too, eat a peace wafer before the Christmas meal.

In Christian churches in Lebanon, the priest repeats the words of the angels' message to the shepherds and touches the hand of the person at his right. This *salaam,* or peace token, then passes from hand to hand throughout the church.

Whether or not we believe in angels, their Christmas message of peace on earth and goodwill to men is one that most of us are glad to hear.

The Shepherds

"Let us now go even unto Bethlehem, and see this thing which is come to pass," said the shepherds of the Bible after the Christmas angels had disappeared.

The humble shepherds, no less than the Three Kings, have inspired painters and poets, and have found their way into beautiful Christmas carols.

The sight of shepherds sleeping by their flocks on the hills outside the town of Greccio gave St. Francis of Assisi his idea for the first live nativity scene. And ever since, people have enjoyed dressing in shepherds' costumes to act out the ancient Christmas story.

In the Mexican town of San Miguel de Allende, floats are paraded through the streets showing tableaux of the Nativity. There are live sheep and goats, and singing children in shepherds' garb.

67

In Tachira, Venezuela, people go from house to house on Christmas Eve dressed as shepherds and shepherdesses. In the Andes mountains of South America and in villages of Mexico, Panama, and the rest of Central America, children in shepherds' costumes perform a dance in the aisles at the church.

The Mexicans have a Christmas play, *Los Pastores,* meaning the shepherds. Performed in villages or on ranches by traveling actors, it is a folk version of a miracle play brought to the New World by the Spanish conquerors. In it the devil tries to keep the shepherds from going to Bethlehem. The shepherds win out, kneeling at the end before the Christ Child, *El Niño.*

68

In towns of northern Brazil there are shepherdesses in the play instead of shepherds, and a gypsy who tries to kidnap the holy child.

For nine nights, beginning on December 16, Mexicans and many Mexican-Americans visit one another's homes to act out *Las Posadas,* an episode from *Los Pastores.* Houses are gay with lilies, Spanish moss, evergreens, and paper lanterns, ready for the knock of the visiting family.

In Los Angeles, Mexican-Americans carry figures of Joseph and Mary from door to door. Behind them comes a troop of children and grownups, carrying lighted candles and shepherds' crooks.

Christmas Creatures

Santa Claus did not always travel by reindeer. Until the nineteenth century, as St. Nicholas, he had ridden a donkey, a horse, or in a sky chariot drawn by horses.

But no animal could serve Santa better than the reindeer. Reindeer can draw sledge-loads at a speed of twelve to fifteen miles an hour for hours at a time. Without their reindeer, the people of Lapland would have no transportation in that barren region of Scandinavia above the Arctic Circle.

Other Scandinavians may have brought the idea of Christmas reindeer to the United States. No one knows this for sure. But almost everyone knows Dancer, Prancer, Donder, Blitzen, and the other merry reindeer in Dr. Clement Moore's famous poem of 1823. And reindeer have galloped, to the jingle of bells, through every Christmas since then.

Whether miniature or lifesize, on greeting cards, in shop windows or on rooftops, reindeer are a symbol of Christmas merrymaking.

Camels represent one of the religious traditions of Christmas. In Spain, Mexico, Argentina, Brazil, and Puerto Rico, children are told that they bear the Three Kings with their gifts for children. And children remember the camels, putting hay or grass for them under their beds, on the roof, or before the door.

In southern Syria the Youngest Camel himself bestows the gifts. According to a Syrian Christmas tale, when the young camel was too weary to walk farther, he fell down, and was blessed by the Christ Child.

Children awaiting the camels never see them any more than we see reindeer, but they wake up to find gifts in place of the hay or grass.

Peasants of central Europe feed their hens and geese wheat that has been blessed at church at Christmas to protect them from evil. In some areas the last sheaf of corn at the harvest was once dressed like a woman—the Corn Mother. On Christmas Eve, a wreath made from the ears of the mother sheaf were put in the manger to make the cattle thrive.

Rooted in ancient magic, customs like these found their way into Christmas early. St. Francis of Assisi gave them further meaning. Because Christ was born in a stable, St. Francis taught, all animals should share in the plenty of Christmas.

Since then, farmers of Europe have given their cattle and horses extra rations at Christmas, and choice bits from the family table. English horses sometimes received a drink of ale.

In parts of Germany the cat, the dog, the canary, and even the mice in a household were all allowed to peek at the Christmas tree. No housewife wanted cobwebs in the room, so spiders were kept out, according to one legend.

Finally, one Christmas, the spiders complained to the Christ Child, who let them in. Down from the attic and up from the cellar they crept. And when they had seen all they could from the floor, they started up the tree, draping the branches with filmy webs. At a touch from the Christ Child the cobwebs turned to golden tinsel.

Spanish people say that one should be especially kind to cows in memory of the cattle whose breath warmed the infant Jesus.

The animals, so the legends go, have Christmas customs of their own. Sheep walk in procession out of respect for the glad tidings the shepherds received. Bees hum a Christmas carol. Roosters crow all night. Farm animals kneel in their stalls, and for one hour on Christmas Eve, all animals can speak.

Christmas Feasting

Good things to eat and drink have been part of holidays throughout history. In many churches, religious holidays are known as feast days. Christmas, like the others, has its own special foods and delicacies.

Christmas dinner in the United States usually means roast turkey, with cranberry sauce and hot vegetables, followed by plum pudding or mince pie, nuts, fruits, and candies.

In Europe turkeys were unknown until the sixteenth century, when Spanish explorers brought some there from Mexico. Even then it was only one of many meat dishes. Most families ate roast goose, roast beef, roast pig, or meat pies at the holiday dinner. On Christmas tables in castles and manor houses there were roast hares, pigs, turkeys, swans, geese, and—choicest of all—roast peacock and boar's head.

74

Long before Christian times, the boar, or wild pig, was sacred to the Druids. They believed that man had learned to plow by seeing the boar dig its tusks into the earth. At the winter solstice, they offered a boar's head to the goddess Frigga.

At Yuletide, the Norsemen ate boar flesh to honor the Sun Boar. The gods in their dwelling place, Valhalla, were said to feast on it all the time.

King Henry VIII of England established it as a Christmas dish. Draped with rosemary and laurel, the boar's head was borne in to the singing of choristers and the playing of minstrels. In the mouth was a lemon, the symbol of plenty. A man of outstanding virtue and courage was chosen to carve it.

Today at Queens College in Oxford, British students eat boar meat, or brawn, at Christmas. As the meat is served, they sing "The Boar's Head Carol."

Next important at medieval English Christmas feasts was roasted peacock. The brilliant feathers wrapped back in place, the crested head erect, the peacock was served by the most distinguished or charming lady.

Knights of the court went up, one by one, to take a Peacock Vow. Each pledged brave deeds on behalf of his lord and lady.

Sometimes, in place of roast peacock, there was peacock pie, with the bird's head and tail feathers extending outward on either side.

Few have tasted peacock pie, but everyone has heard of Jack Horner's Christmas pie. A mince pie, it has topped off Christmas dinners for five hundred years.

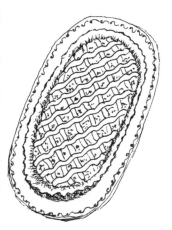

Mince pie was once made of chopped partridges, pheasants, hares, and later of chopped beef. As time went on, cooks began adding suet, sugar, apples, molasses, raisins, currants, and spices.

The first such pies were oblong, a symbol of the manger. The latticework crust stood for the hayrack. The apples in the mincemeat expressed a hope for good crops in the coming year. The spices recalled the gifts of the wise men from the East.

Kings and nobles boasted about the size of their Christmas pies. A pie baked for one English lord took two bushels of flour, twenty pounds of butter, and measured nine feet around the edge. Among the wild game in it were seven blackbirds.

So prized were the pies that someone stayed up all night on Christmas Eve to watch them. The poet Robert Herrick spoke of it like this:

Come guard the Christmas-pie,
That the Thief, though ne'er so sly,
With his Flesh-hooks don't come nigh
                    to catch it.

Eating the pies was believed to bring good luck. For especially good luck, people ate one pie a day between Christmas and Twelfth Night. Leftover pies were given to the poor.

Plum pudding, as we know it, dates from about 1670. It began as a thick plum porridge made of meat broth, chopped cows' tongues, raisins, fruit juice, wine, and spices. The word plum meant to rise or swell, as the raisins do when cooked.

At medieval English Christmas banquets there were often twelve different courses. Between each course, sugar statues of the wise men or holy family, called *Subtleties,* were placed on the table to be eaten as dessert.

Before the feast began, the guests drank from the festive wassail bowl of hot spiced ale. Roasted apples floated on the surface, and sometimes egg and cream were added. "Wassail!" each guest would cry, meaning "Here's to you!" or "To your health!"

Saxon ancestors of the English had drunk ale from the skulls of their enemies. King Henry VIII is said to have made the wassail bowl a Christmas custom. The royal bowl was richly ornamented, and decorated with greens.

During the Twelve Days of Christmas, young men with simpler bowls went from house to house, singing carols and hoping for treats.

Children went "gooding," singing "Here we come a-wassailing," a carol that is still sung today.

English farmers carried the wassail bowl to the barn and drank toasts to the health of their cattle. Some even wassailed their beehives, their trees, and fields.

In certain apple-raising districts in England, groups of men still fire shotguns through the tree branches on Twelfth Night, and pour cider around the roots. A Christmas custom today, it was once a magical rite to frighten evil spirits away and encourage the growth of fruit.

In countries like Czechoslovakia and Rumania, there is often a roast suckling pig with an apple in its mouth for Christmas. Germans, Hungarians, Belgians, and Dutch are more likely to have roast goose.

Finnish families enjoy a steam bath, the *sauna,* on Christmas Eve. Then they sit down to a feast that includes barley porridge, almonds, and fish. In Norway, Denmark, and Sweden, too, the main dish is usually fish. People of Lapland dine on reindeer meat.

In Central and South America, besides turkey, chicken, and pork, there is a great variety of other foods. Mexicans enjoy Christmas tamales, while Brazilians add fried shrimp.

In the African Republic of Ghana, groups of Christian families buy cows, sheep, and goats to be slaughtered for the Christmas feast. Among Christians of Abyssinia a favorite Christmas dish is raw meat.

Roast beef or fowl is the main dish at the holiday dinner in Australia. There Christmas comes in the summer and people spend the rest of the day at the beaches.

Most American families have the dinner on Christmas Day, but those of Scandinavian or German stock prefer Christmas Eve. Members of Greek Orthodox or Russian churches eat Christmas dinner on January 6.

Some Christians fast for one or more weeks before Christmas. In Iran, Christmas is called the Little Feast, while Easter is the Great Feast. From the first day of December until the 25th, Iranian Christians eat no meat, eggs, milk, or cheese. On Christmas morning, after an early mass, the fast ends and many people eat *harasa,* a chicken stew.

During the Puritan ban on Christmas many New Englanders fasted the day before.

The fast in Russia and Poland always ended with the first star on Christmas Eve. In memory of the manger, the table for the Christmas feast in Russia was covered with straw.

In Lithuania, a snowy white cloth, used only on Christmas Eve, covered a layer of fresh hay. Everyone at the table drew out a straw. An older person was happy to draw a long

straw, for that meant a longer life. A young girl hoped for a short straw, meaning that she would marry soon.

On Christmas Day in 1492, Christopher Columbus' ship, the *Santa Maria,* struck a sand bank in the West Indies. A fleet of canoes promptly arrived from the island of Guarico to help. The following day the island's chief took Columbus ashore and served him a dinner of shrimps, cassavi, and nutritious roots.

At Jamestown, one stormy Christmas more than a hundred years later, Captain John Smith wrote of keeping the holiday among the "salvages," as he called the Indians.

"We weere never more merry," he wrote, "nor fed on more plenty of good Oysters, Fish, Flesh, Wild Fowl and good bread, nor never had better fires in England."

The Indians told the Pilgrims that the red berries in the bogs around Plymouth were good to eat. From then on, turkey was often eaten with cranberry sauce, one of the few native American Christmas foods. Most were brought here by the English, Dutch, Germans, Scandinavians, Irish, French, Italians, Russians, Polish, Mexicans, Puerto Ricans, and all the others who make up what we call Americans.

In California or the Southwest, one may see a Mexican *piñata,* a large fragile jar made to look like a clown, a bullfighter, or a rooster. Blindfolded children take turns trying to break it until finally a shower of candy and fruit descends.

French bakers make delicious Yule logs. Italians bake *panettone,* the tall mound of bread flavored with citron and raisins. Germans bake gingerbread men and hard spicy cookies called *Pfefferkuchen.* From Germany or Austria comes marzipan, made of sugar and almond paste, in the shapes of strawberries, bananas, apples, or vegetables.

At Christmas people like a feeling of plenty. And they enjoy sharing it with their relatives, their friends, or with people they may not even know.

Christmas Bells

Weeks before Christmas we hear the jingle of bells and see their shapes all around us.

Hundreds of years before the first Christmas, bells had announced happy as well as sad events. All major religions except the Mohammedan have clashed cymbals or rung bells. Primitive tribes of Africa or North America have shaken seed-filled rattles in religious ceremonies.

The first bells rang in ancient Asia, the largest of these in China. In one district, a certain governor sat in his palace beneath a huge bell. From it a rope stretched out along the highway for a mile. Anyone treated unjustly was free to tug on it.

The high priests of the ancient Hebrews wore robes decorated with tiny golden bells and rang hand bells at their ceremonies. The early Egyptians rang bells at the feast of their god Osiris. In ancient Rome a bell hung before the temple of Jupiter.

During the sixth century, bells appeared in Christian churches. On Christmas Eve or Christmas day they announced the birthday of Jesus.

By the Middle Ages, bells had become an established part of the Christmas season. The poor rang hand bells on the streets and collected alms, just as men in Santa Claus suits do today to aid the needy.

Bells in churches were once named and baptized. Their pealing was said to drive away fiends, goblins, and lightning. The bells could also put out fires, people believed, divert a thunderstorm, and purify the air after an epidemic.

At the moment of Jesus' birth, legends explain, the devil died. A church in Yorkshire, England, at one time made a ceremony of it. From midnight on Christmas Eve until one o'clock, the bells tolled the "Devil's Knell."

When the Puritans ruled England, town criers rang loud hand bells as they forbade people to observe Christmas.

St. Nicholas carried a hand bell, and Befana rang a bell as she entered Italian chimneys.

In certain places in Europe people used to put their heads to the ground on Christmas Eve and declare they heard bells ringing. Such a place, they declared, was once a valley, swallowed up by an earthquake on Christmas Eve.

Bells have also appealed to the imagination of poets and composers. Edgar Allen Poe called them "the opera of the steeples." Charles Wesley is said to have composed the carol "Hark the Herald Angels Sing" after listening to Christmas chimes.

Bells were never so welcome as at Christmas, when they pealed forth the message of peace and joy. Out of fashion for a time, they ring today as never before.

Weeks before the holiday, chimes set the Christmas mood. A chime is a set of movable bells struck by a hammer or rung by hand to play a tune.

A carillon has as many as 70 bells. It is tuned more exactly, and often played from a keyboard. Belgium has a special school for the art. Sometimes the melody is called a carillon.

The instrument grew out of the fifteenth century Belgian *voorslag*—a set of bells in a clock tower that played a tune before it struck the hour.

In the Low Countries, one town or city

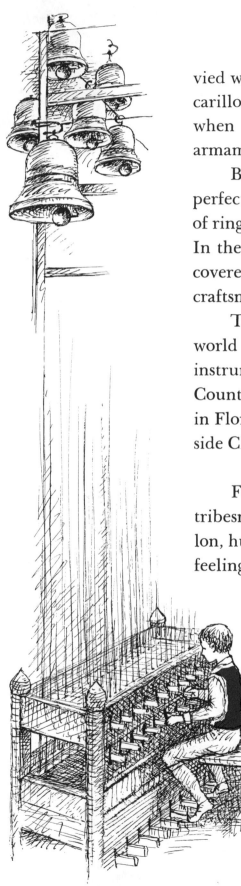

vied with another in the size and quality of its carillon. Then, in the eighteenth century, when carillons were melted down to make armaments, the art declined.

Bell players of England, meanwhile, had perfected the art of *change ringing*. A group of ringers struck the bells in a changing order. In the nineteenth century, the English rediscovered the secrets of Flemish and Dutch craftsmen, and revived the carillon.

Today carillon-playing is the finest the world has known. There are now at least 450 instruments. One hundred are in the Low Countries. A famous one is the Singing Tower in Florida at Lake Wales. Another is at Riverside Church in New York City.

From the rattling gourds of primitive tribesmen to the bell music of a modern carillon, human beings have used sound to express feeling—at Christmas the feeling of joy.

Christmas Colors

The red of holly berries, of a Santa Claus or Father Christmas outfit; the green of fir trees; the gold of candlelight or stars; the whiteness of snowy fields. These are the colors of Christmas.

Human beings have always been cheered or excited by warm colors like red or yellow, and soothed by cool ones like blue or green.

Red, the color of greatest excitement, is also the special color for December. In the language of religious symbols, it stands for fire, blood, and charity.

At Christmas people of like blood enjoy gathering together. And, wherever they are, people are likely to be their kindest and most charitable.

Green is a symbol of nature, a symbol of youth and the hope of eternal life. And Christmas is a feast of hope, with a newborn child as its central symbol.

White, as a religious symbol, stands for light, purity, joy, and glory. We see it in the robes of Christmas angels, in Santa's beard and suit trimmings, in Christmas snow or in snowflakes.

In northern Europe and America, snow covers the ground at Christmas. In southern California roses are blooming. On Florida beaches people are sunbathing. Yet, in warm places like these, snow spangles the windows of stores and lies under many Christmas trees. It is artificial snow, but a link with the northern Yuletide.

Gold stands for sunlight and radiance. It is the color of shining Christmas stars, sparkling tinsel, glowing candles, or blazing electric bulbs.

Pagans, becoming Christian, saw the new god as they had the sun—a radiant being who lighted the world. Artists through the ages have shown Christ in a pool of light, or with a bright halo around his head.

Regardless of religion, almost everyone enjoys the colors of Christmas: cheerful red, hopeful green, snowy white, and dazzling gold.

Christmas Cards

Christmas after Christmas, bulging mail sacks carry tons of cards to friends and relatives all over the world.

On the cards are the many symbols of Christmas—holly, reindeer, candles, camels, angels, shepherds, and all the others.

The sending of printed Christmas greetings began in England. There, schoolboys away from home had been writing Christmas letters to their parents on paper printed with Bible scenes or with birds and flowers. In their best penmanship, hoping for generous Christmas gifts, they reported on their progress at school.

Grownups sometimes wrote Christmas verses to friends on similar paper or on small calling cards.

In the 1840's true Christmas cards appeared. One designed by William Egley, a young engraver's apprentice, is said by some to have been the first.

Christmas was once more a merry holiday by that time. Queen Victoria encouraged it. Charles Dickens, with his story *A Christmas Carol* and other holiday stories, helped revive

it, too. Enjoying the new warmer Christmas spirit that was in the air, William Egley wanted to share it with others.

His card, now in the British Museum, shows people at Christmas dinner and other people dancing, singing carols, and giving food to the poor. Each scene is in a separate panel. William had a hundred copies made and sent them to his friends.

Around the same time, Sir Henry Cole had the artist John Horsley design a card. A thousand copies were printed, colored by hand, and sold for a shilling apiece.

Both cards were bordered with a trellis and grapevines. One panel of Horsley's card shows a family drinking wine. This caused so much stir that all of London began talking about it. Soon a number of companies were printing Christmas cards. Designed by famous artists and printed in lavish color, they were too costly for most people.

In twenty or thirty years a new way of printing color lowered the prices, while a new postal system in England lowered mailing costs. Now, almost anyone could send Christmas cards.

On these were cupids, robins, flowers,

holly or mistletoe, and, sometimes, Father Christmas with a troop of children. There were joke cards as well as serious ones. For those who could afford it, there were frosted, gilded, or jeweled cards, some painted by hand on plush or satin.

Later, scenes of winter on Christmas cards gave way to springtime or summer. The children's book illustrator Kate Greenaway designed a number like this.

Soon, the Christmas card found its way to the United States. In 1874 a German immigrant named Louis Prang in Roxbury, Massachusetts, began printing beautiful cards that people liked. Within ten years he was selling several million a year. Hundreds of other companies sprang up, until the Christmas card business became the gigantic one it is today.

Different countries have very different cards. On a German Christmas card there might be a rose, on an English one, a blue robin. Spanish or Puerto Rican cards may feature the Three Kings or the minstrels who wander about the streets at Christmas, playing carols.

More people, Christian and non-Christian alike, take part in sending Christmas cards

than in any other Christmas custom. And more cards are mailed at Christmas than on any other single holiday.

Most people choose printed cards. Some design cards of their own and have them printed. Some, who send only a few and want each one to be special, create a special card for each person.

Some cards are religious. Many are not. Some are not even true Christmas cards. With wintry scenes and no mention of Christmas, they are more like cards celebrating midwinter—a link with our ancient ancestors. On others the picture is from a work of art, the message a wish for good luck, for peace and joy.

Whatever the card, it is a way of telling people that we remember them, care what happens to them, feel grateful toward them, think they are fun, like them, or love them.

An exchange of Christmas cards often helps keep alive a friendship between people too far apart to see each other. The simple gesture of sending a card sometimes mends a broken friendship. For Christmas is a season for reaching out to others and sharing warmth and joy.

I heard a bird sing
In the dark of December
A magical thing
And sweet to remember.

—OLIVER HERFORD

The blazing log, sparkling Christmas lights, the Christ Child—all these express joy in the triumph of light and warmth over darkness and cold.

Evergreens, "the plants that do not die," link us with all of nature. They express the hope that life will go on and on.

Santa Claus and other Christmas gift bringers are the spirit of loving and giving; the angels, the spirit of peaceful and kindly feeling.

These and the other symbols, with their reminders of our common ancestors, show that Christmas is more than a festival of one particular religion. It is a celebration of the deepest and best of human feelings—a festival to life itself.

Christmas Stories and Poems

ASSOCIATION FOR CHILDHOOD EDUCATION INTERNATIONAL. Literature Committee, editors. *Told Under the Christmas Tree.* New York: The Macmillan Company, 1948. Stories by Beatrix Potter, Kenneth Grahame, Louisa May Alcott, Ruth Sawyer, Ludwig Bemelmans, Marguerite de Angeli, and others. Includes several Hanukkah stories.

DALGLEISH, Alice, editor. *Christmas Stories Old and New.* New York: Charles Scribner's Sons, 1962. Includes the first Christmas, Christmas in old-time America, and Christmas in many lands.

EATON, Anne, compiler. *The Animals' Christmas.* New York: The Viking Press, 1944. Stories, poems, and carols in which animals have important roles.

EATON, Anne, compiler. *Welcome Christmas: A Garland of Poems.* New York: The Viking Press, 1955. Some old, some more modern, all ageless.

HAZELTINE, Alice I., and SMITH, Elva S., editors. *The Christmas Book of Legends and Stories.* New York: Lothrop, Lee & Shepard Co., 1944. More than one hundred poems, stories, legends, and plays.

REEVES, James, compiler. *The Christmas Book.* New York: E. P. Dutton & Co., 1968. Ballads, carols, legends, modern tales and verse, ranging from Shakespeare and Herrick to Dylan Thomas.

ROLLINS, Charlemae, compiler. *Christmas Gif'.* Chicago: Follett Publishing Company, 1963. Stories, poems, and songs written by and about black people.

Index